Amphibians and Reptiles

A Compare and Contrast Book

by Katharine Hall

Amphibians and reptiles are two different classes of animals. Scientists who study them are called herpetologists.

There are three main types of amphibians.

frogs and toads

salamanders and newts

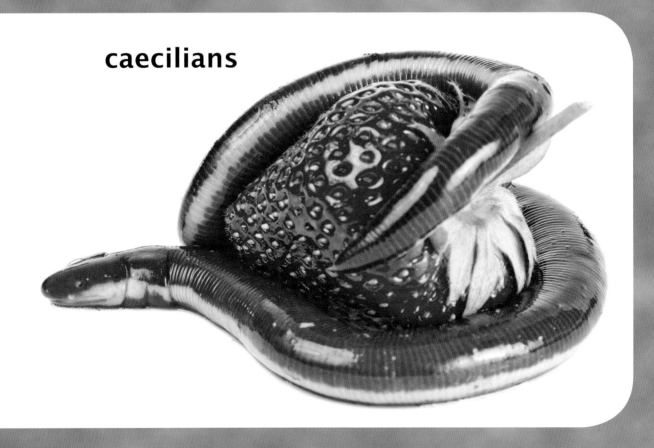

caecilians

There are four different kinds of reptiles.

crocodylians

tuatara

lizards, worm lizards, and snakes

turtles and tortoises

Amphibians and reptiles are cold-blooded.

This olympic salamander stays moist and cool by resting on wet earth.

This American alligator keeps warm by resting in the sun.

Most amphibians hatch
from eggs in the water.

Most reptiles hatch from eggs on land.

When amphibians hatch, they live in the water as tadpoles. As they grow, their bodies change form in a process called "metamorphosis."

When reptiles are young,
they look like small versions
of their adult selves.

Amphibians absorb oxygen from the water when they are young . . .

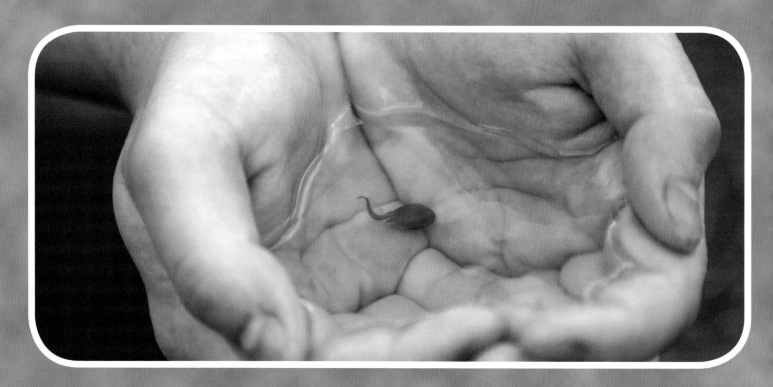

. . . and from the air when they are adults.

Reptiles breathe oxygen from
the air their entire lives.

Most amphibians have moist, smooth skin.

Reptiles have dry scales.

There are many different types of amphibians. Some, like this poison dart frog, are poisonous to predators that try to touch or eat them.

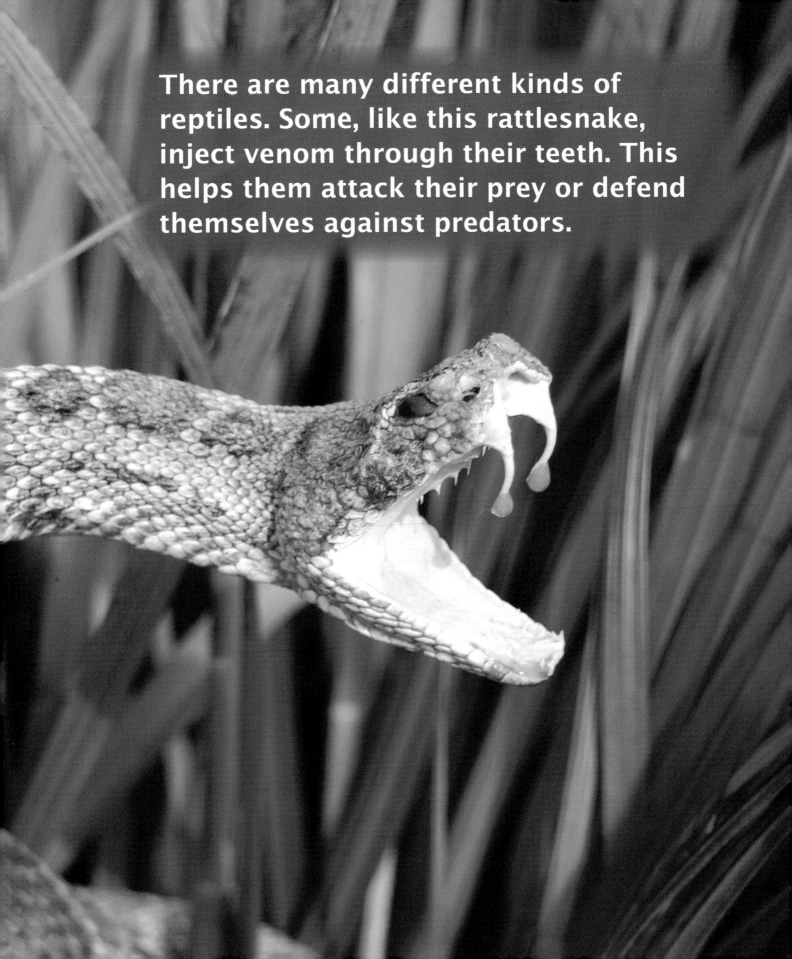

There are many different kinds of reptiles. Some, like this rattlesnake, inject venom through their teeth. This helps them attack their prey or defend themselves against predators.

Amphibians and reptiles live all around us.

For Creative Minds

Vertebrate Classes

All living things can be sorted into groups based on what they have in common. Scientists call this practice of sorting **taxonomy**. Animals can be divided into vertebrate animals and invertebrate animals. A **vertebrate animal** has a backbone (spine or spinal column). Humans, dogs, sharks, owls, snakes, and salamanders are all vertebrate animals. **Invertebrate animals** don't have a backbone. Worms, slugs, spiders, insects, squid, and oysters are all invertebrate animals.

Vertebrate animals can be sorted into five **classes**: fish, amphibians, reptiles, birds, and mammals.

Fishes:
- most have scales covered with a thin layer of slime
- gills to breathe
- babies are either born alive or hatch from eggs
- cold-blooded

Amphibians:
- most have soft, moist skin
- most hatchlings are called larvae or tadpoles and live in water, using gills or skin to breathe
- as they grow, they develop legs and lungs and move onto land
- cold-blooded

Reptiles:
- dry scales or plates
- lungs to breathe
- babies are either born alive or hatch from leathery eggs
- cold-blooded

Birds:
- feathers
- lungs to breathe
- hatch from eggs
- warm-blooded

Peachtree

Mammals:
- hair, fur, whiskers, or quills at some point in their lives
- lungs to breathe
- most give birth to live young
- produce milk to feed young
- warm-blooded

Amphibian or Reptile Sorting

Use clues from the book to determine which of the animals below are amphibians and which are reptiles.

American alligator

garter snake

loggerhead sea turtle

olympic salamander

poison dart frog

Puerto Rican crested toad

Texas horned lizard

tuatara

woodhouse toad

Amphibians: olympic salamander, poison dart frog, Puerto Rican crested toad, woodhouse toad
Reptiles: American alligator, garter snake, loggerhead sea turtle, Texas horned lizard, tuatara

Herpetology

Herpetology is the study of amphibians and reptiles (herps). Herpetologists can work in universities, museums, zoos, conservation programs, rehabilitation centers, ecology programs, nature centers, and veterinary offices. If you think herpetology might be for you, it is never too early to get started! Read about amphibians and reptiles. Visit local nature centers, zoos, or parks to find out more about the animals in your area. Volunteer at nature centers and other places where you can gain experience and work alongside professionals.

Field work is an important part of science. But before you go looking for herps in your area, find out if there are any venomous or poisonous ones you should avoid. Learn to recognize the dangerous animals so you can keep yourself safe and only approach the harmless ones.

When you are looking for herps, move slowly. Watch for a quickly darting herp looking for cover, or for motionless ones under logs and other debris. Listen for the rustle of a camouflaged animal moving through the grass or other plants. Many herps like to hide under logs, rocks, and leaves. **Never stick your hand in places you can't see.** Use a tool like a garden hoe or a stick to turn over the leaves or sticks and see what is underneath. If you move any rocks or logs while looking for herps, make sure to put them back in their place so you don't damage any animal's habitat.

If you catch any amphibians or reptiles, keep them only long enough to observe them and then release them back where they came from. Because you will be doing all of your observations in the field, it is important to be prepared. Pack a "research kit" with tools that can help you observe and record information about the animals you find:

- A notebook. Write information about the animals you found and the habitats where you found them. Include the date, exact location, habitat, weather, and behavior.
- A camera. Take pictures of both their dorsal (back) and ventral (stomach) sides.
- A net. Use this to catch small, harmless herps. Do not take the tadpoles out of the water—at this stage in their lives, they cannot breathe air and would die.
- A magnifying glass. Closely examine the animals you catch. Pay attention to the colors and patterns of their markings so you can identify them later.
- A small ruler or flexible cloth tape. Measure the animal and make notes.
- Plastic bags or jars. These can help hold your herp while you make your observations. Poke holes in the bag or in the lid of the jar so that the animal can breathe.

Amphibian Life Cycle Sequencing

Put the amphibian life cycle events in order to spell the scrambled word.

R

When the eggs hatch, little tadpoles or larvae swim out. They have dark, oval bodies and swim by moving their long tails. They breathe oxygen from the water.

G

The legs continue to grow and the gills disappear. At this point, the amphibians look like miniature adults and can leave the water.

S

Over time, the amphibian continues to mature. Eventually it is an adult and will be able to reproduce. After mating, a female amphibian will lay her eggs in fresh water.

F
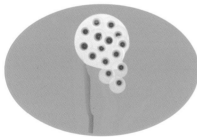
An adult amphibian lays eggs in fresh water. The eggs do not have a hard shell. They are small and soft, surrounded by layers of jelly that protects the tiny embryo growing inside.

O

As the tadpoles grow, they begin to develop legs. Many amphibians keep their tails for their whole life, but in frogs and toads, the tail begins to shrink. Their lungs develop and they start to visit the surface of the water to breathe air.

Answer: FROGS

To Terry and Ellen, for holding the herps while I took notes.—KH

Thanks to Dr. Kenneth L. Krysko, Division of Herpetology at the Florida Museum of Natural History, for reviewing the accuracy of the information in this book.

Library of Congress Cataloging-in-Publication Data

Hall, Katharine, 1989- author.
  Amphibians and reptiles : a compare and contrast book / by Katharine Hall.
    pages cm. -- (Compare and contrast book)
  Audience: Ages 4-8.
  Includes bibliographical references.
  ISBN 978-1-62855-551-6 (english hardcover) -- ISBN 978-1-62855-560-8 (english pbk.) -- ISBN 978-1-62855-578-3 (english downloadable ebook) -- ISBN 978-1-62855-596-7 (english interactive dual-language ebook) -- ISBN 978-1-62855-569-1 (spanish pbk.) -- ISBN 978-1-62855-587-5 (spanish downloadable ebook) -- ISBN 978-1-62855-605-6 (spanish interactive dual-language ebook) 1. Amphibians--Juvenile literature. 2. Reptiles--Juvenile literature. I. Title. II. Series: Compare and contrast book.
  QL644.2.H34 2015
  597--dc23
                                    2015009084

Translated into Spanish: *Anfibios y Reptiles: Un libro de comparación y contraste*

Lexile® Level: 690L

key phrases for educators: amphibians, animal classification, compare & contrast, complete metamorphosis, life cycles, metamorphosis, reptiles, vertebrate classification

Bibliography:

"Amphibians, Reptiles and Fish." National Wildlife Federation. Accessed June 2014. Web.

Collins, Joseph T., Roger Conant, Roger Tory Peterson, and Isabelle Hunt Conant. A Field Guide to Reptiles and Amphibians: Eastern and Central North America. Peterson Field Guides. Boston: Houghton Mifflin Harcourt, 1998.

"Rules and Tools for the Young Herpetologist." Virginia Herpetological Society. Accessed June 2014. Web.

Photo Credits:

Thanks to author Katharine Hall and her husband, Terry Hall, for supplying the photographs indicated below. Thanks to the following photographers for releasing their images into the public domain or for making them available via Shutterstock.

red poison dart frog sitting on green leaf—Dirk Ercken, Shutterstock
turtle—Terry Hall
cheat mountain salamander—Ryan Hagerty, USFWS
"I think I've Got Something"—Steve Hillebrand, USFWS
snake demonstration—Steve Hillebrand, USFWS
man with turtle—Katharine Hall
frog in hands—Terry Hall
river frog on a branch—Mark A. Musselman, USFWS
cheat mountain salamander—Ryan Hagerty, USFWS
fish caecilian—Kamnuan, Shutterstock
American alligator—Steve Hillebrand, USFWS
tuatara—Andrew McMillan
collared lizard—Lawrence Gamble, USFWS
painted turtle—W.L. Franch, USFWS
olympic salamander—John and Karen Hollingsworth, USFWS
alligator on the bank of pond at St. Marks National Wildlife Refuge—Steve Hillebrand, USFWS
frog egg mass—Pete Pattavina, USFWS
sea turtle egg relocation—Jennifer Strickland, USFWS
red legged frog—Mark R. Jennings, USFWS
two tadpoles in water—Tom Tetzner, USFWS
loggerhead sea turtle—Peter Leahy, Shutterstock
baby loggerhead heading towards ocean—Steve Hillebrand, USFWS
small tadpoles in the hands of a man—Alex Kalashnikov, Shutterstock
longtail salamander—Ryan Hagerty, USFWS
Texas horned lizard—Steve Hillebrand, USFWS
frogs—Peter Griffin
alligator—Tammy Sue
red poison dart frog sitting on green leaf—Dirk Ercken, Shutterstock
sneaky snake in grass—Maria Dryfhout, Shutterstock
turtle in Hands—Katharine Hall
garter snake—Kim Newberg
Puerto Rican crested toad—Jan P. Zegarra, USFWS
woodhouse toad—Gary M. Stolz, USFWS
Lake Erie water snake—Megan Seymour, USFWS
eastern indigo snake—James Rickard, USFWS

Manufactured in China, June 2015
This product conforms to CPSIA 2008
First Printing

Arbordale Publishing
Mt. Pleasant, SC 29464
www.ArbordalePublishing.com